AF476887

LMS Days

LMS Days

WD & DS Cooper

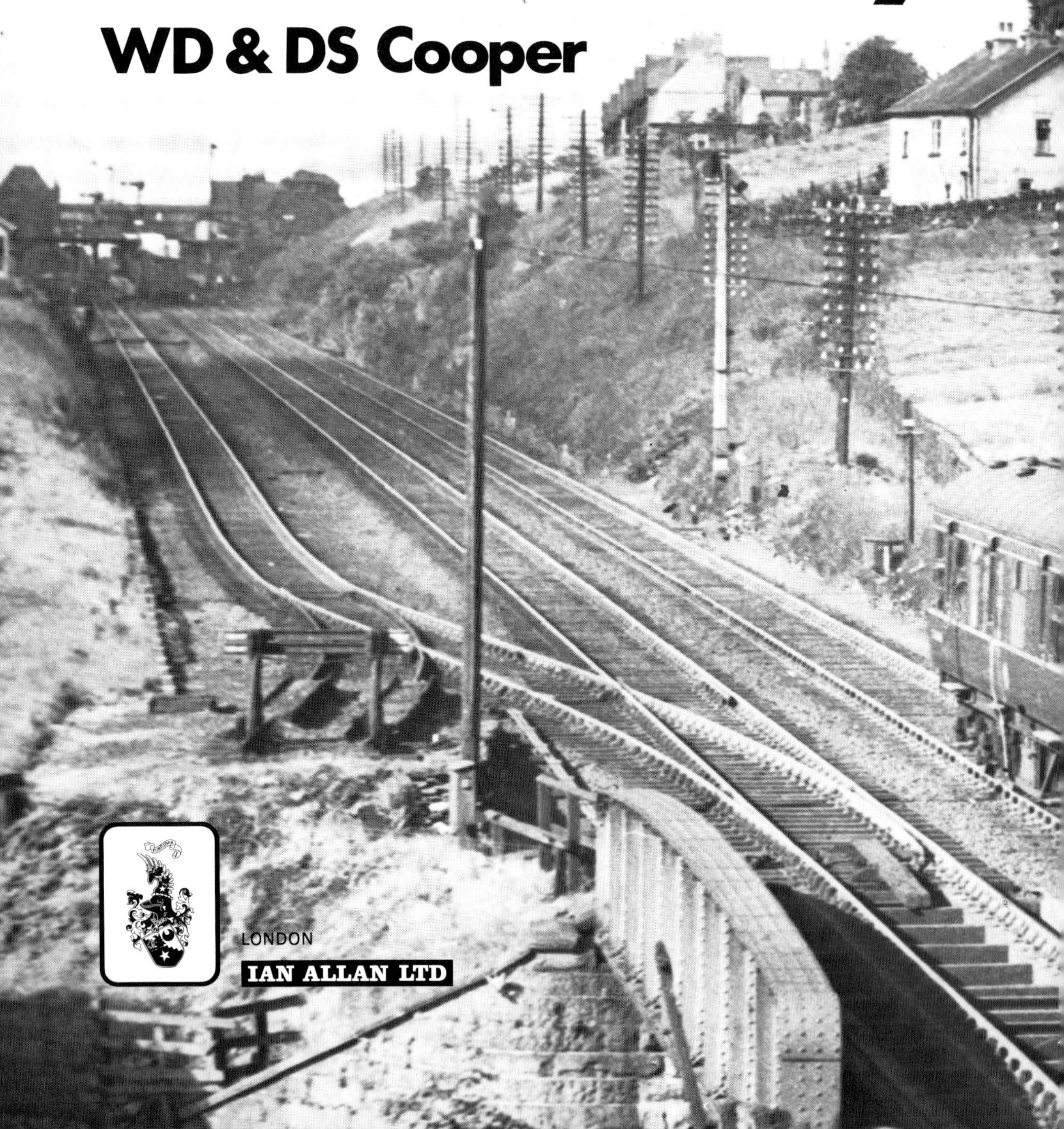

First published 1979

ISBN 0 7110 0914 7

Published by Ian Allan Ltd, Shepperton, Surrey; and printed in the United Kingdom by Ian Allan Printing Ltd

Previous page: An Engineer's Inspection Coach heads south from Tebay in August 1947 in the charge of Class 2 No 488.

Below: 'Royal Scot' No 6130 *The West Yorkshire Regiment* heads south on the 1 in 125 gradient north of Shap on a July afternoon in 1938.

It has been a conscious decision to include in this volume photographs of historic interest which might, in other circumstances, have been excluded on grounds of quality. It is hoped the reader will accept the consequent reduction in the production standards of some plates.

Introduction

Born within sight of the Patricroft locomotive depot and living in that locality for many years, my interest in the railway began at an early age. In addition I had in me what could be called a 'bump' for engineering, and this helped to make the steam locomotive of special interest. As soon as I could use any form of tool I was ready to make things, and this led on to the building of scale steam locomotives, a hobby which has occupied many hours of work over many years. The same inclination led me to take up employment with a local firm which built steam engines, albeit stationary ones.

Very naturally, any photographs of engines were much prized; I gradually became interested in the art of railway photography, and was joined in the 1930s by my brother. Well do we remember pleasant outings searching for suitable locations and subjects on which to practice the art, although with rather limited success at first.

We quickly discovered the unsuitability of cameras then in our possession, with inadequate lenses and shutters; not to mention the frustrations of certain second-hand equipment which, as we learnt the hard way, had inherent malfunctions not always easy to rectify. Although the facts will be well known to experienced photographers, some readers may be interested in our experience with different types of cameras and shutters. I suppose the first lesson learnt was that a camera with a shutter giving a top speed of $\frac{1}{100}$sec was quite inadequate for anything other than 'portraits' of static subjects. Some success was enjoyed with a Compur shutter which gave a minimum exposure of $\frac{1}{250}$sec but this left much to be desired. Being located between the elements of the camera lens, this type of shutter exposes the whole of the negative at once, and since an object moving at 60mph advances over four inches in $\frac{1}{250}$sec it follows that some part of the scene recorded will not be sharp — either the train, if the camera is not moved, or the background if the camera is 'panned' as the train passes. The relative sharpness also depends on the angle of the approaching train, becoming progressively less sharp as the angle changes from head-on (when the image on the negative 'grows' comparatively slowly as the train approaches) to a full side shot (when the image of the train on the emulsion is moving very quickly). A Compur Rapid shutter with a minimum exposure of $\frac{1}{500}$sec proved much more satisfactory.

The most suitable shutter is the focal-plane type, which exposes the negative 'a bit at a time' as a slit of variable width in a roller blind travels across the film or plate immediately in front of the emulsion. Shutters of this type are commonly

Above: On the rising gradient through Standish, 'Royal Scot' No 6145 *The Duke of Wellington's Regiment (West Riding)* makes a sustained effort with a northbound express in 1938.

designed for $\frac{1}{1000}$sec and even $\frac{1}{2000}$sec and are used in conjunction with 'fast' lenses in order to pass sufficient light during such brief exposures. However, a little thought will reveal that care is still needed! Depending on which way the slit travels across the emulsion, and at what speed, the overall image can be sharp but distorted. For example, if the slit travels from top to bottom, taking $\frac{1}{250}$sec to get from one side of the film to the other, a train moving at 60mph will have moved forward over four inches, and the resulting photograph will depict it 'leaning forward' — ie, whilst the picture will be sharp, the top of the smokebox will be ahead of the wheels. The aim is to have a shutter with a rapid movement and, if possible, travelling across the negative rather than in a vertical plane in order to make any distortion less obtrusive.

One difficulty encountered in the early days was in the use of a developer which contained metol. The least trace of this chemical on my fingers caused metol poisoning, which had the unpleasant effect of causing the skin to peel off, leaving the fingers extremely tender. Whilst I had to take stringent precautions on this account when working in the dark-room, my brother was quite unaffected by it. Needless to say, an alternative developer without the unpleasant side-effect was used subsequently, and work in the dark-room then became much more enjoyable. My engineering bent was put to good use in 1938 when an enlarger

6

was made; this has done yeoman service over the years and has been used to print the scenes illustrated in this book.

As in all ventures, there were disappointments. One can recall instances when a photograph of a certain train had been planned only to discover, too late, that the shutter had not been wound up, or there was a failure at some stage of the developing process. On other occasions, another train would run past at the crucial moment, obscuring the view. There was a day when this happened three times in succession (the LMS days were busy ones!)

Rightly or wrongly, it was felt at the time that plates gave better results than film (although one has to bear in mind this was about 40 years ago!). This posed the problem of reloading the camera in the open with the help of a 'changing bag'. The object of the exercise was to remove the exposed plate from the holder, replace it with an unused one, making certain that the emulsion was the right way round, avoid getting finger marks on the plates in the process, and avoid exposing them to the least suggestion of light. On a hot, sunny day at the lineside, fumbling around inside the black velvet bag with sticky fingers, this was anything but easy even after much practice, and was guaranteed to cause disappointments from time to time.

Railway photography is not without hazards. However absorbed in a particular subject one became, split-second timing being only one of many factors calling for concentration, it was necessary to be constantly aware of the environment, particularly since the noise of a passing train coincides with the peak of one's effort to secure a good photograph. Fortunately one can recall only minor hazards which befell the photographers, such as an occasion when failure to step high enough over a signal wire resulted in a fall which did nothing to improve the condition of the camera in use at the time!

Acknowledgements must be made to the railway officials of the day. Without the facilities granted in the form of Shed and Walking Permits, few photographs could have been taken and much interesting material could not have been recorded. I was privileged in being allowed to move around without hindrance, particularly as, unlike my brother, I was not a railway employee. Latterly I had my own engineering business, whereas my brother made his career on the railway and was, for a time, a stationmaster in the Manchester Division.

Standing today (1978) on the footbridge spanning what was once Eccles Junction and looking across the vast expanse of now derelict land which was once the scene of bustling activity in and immediately around Patricroft sheds, one can only feel sad. At the same time one feels privileged to have witnessed a unique era of railway history. The amalgamation of the smaller companies, with their numerous classes of locomotive, resulted in 'train spotting' at its best. During the period recorded in this book the whole system was at its zenith with the result that line occupation was intense; the next train was seldom long coming, and one was never sure what surprise was in store when it came into sight. In the LMS days, trains were longer and heavier. It was common to see 17 coaches being hauled up Shap and Beattock, and many drivers would not think twice about taking up 15 unassisted. Similarly on the freight side, trains of 60 loaded coal wagons were anything but unusual. The locomotives of the day advertised these facts! Breathing fire and smoke, one felt they were alive and saying so — a characteristic one feels to be missing in present diesel and electric days.

Garstang   W. D. Cooper

Above: Rebuilt 'Royal Scot' No 6128 *The Lovat Scouts* awaits its turn of duty at Crewe just after the war.

Below: 'Royal Scot' No 6142 *The York and Lancaster Regiment* speeds south on the West Coast main line through Bolton-le-Sands in May 1945.

Above: A photograph taken in August 1939 of 'Royal Scot' No 6124 *London Scottish* on the turntable at Upperby.

Below: Passing Scotforth, south of Lancaster, No 6110 *Grenadier Guardsman* of the 'Royal Scot' class heads an up special in the postwar years.

Above: 'Royal Scot' No 6137 *The Prince Of Wales' Volunteers (South Lancashire)* speeds with an up express near Golborne in August 1946.

Below: A Derby-built 'Royal Scot' No 6163 *Civil Service Rifleman* skirts Morecombe Bay (seen in background) in April 1947.

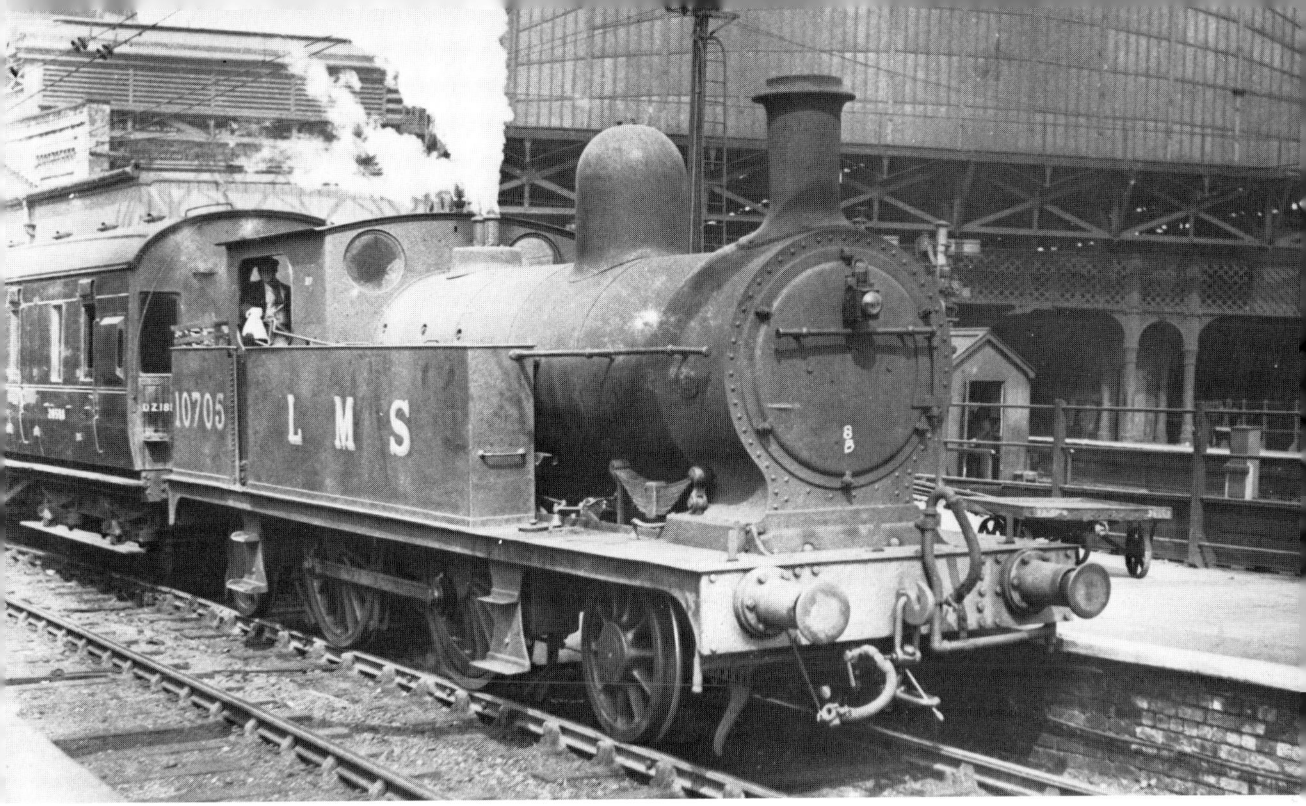

Above: Still at work in the postwar years, ex-L&Y 2-4-2T No 10705 stands in the MSJ&A electric line platform at Manchester London Road.

Below: Ex-L&Y 2-4-2T No 10736 waits outside Newton Heath mpd in the last years of the LMS.

Above: A postwar scene on the L&Y line near Clifton Junction shows another L&Y 2-4-2T, No 10847, at the head of a Manchester-bound local train.

Below: Bunker-end view of ex-L&Y 2-4-2T No 10738 at Newton Heath.

Above: Aspinall 0-6-0 No 12458 on shunting duty at Blackpool in the postwar period.

Below: A pick-up goods north of Golborne is headed by Aspinall 0-6-0 No 12172 on a sunny afternoon in the summer of 1946.

Above: More vintage L&Y as Barton Wright 0-6-0 No 12063 approaches the photographer with freight near Golborne in 1947.

Below: L&Y saddle tanks Nos 11438 and 11424 stand idle in Newton Heath shed on a June day in 1946.

Above right: A Wigan to Manchester local train leaves Walkden (High Level) behind L&Y 2-4-2T No 10923 in September 1945.

Centre right: Hughes 'Crab' 2-6-0 No 2703 heads a southbound stopping train on the West Coast main line near Coppull in July 1938.

Below right: A light goods is trundled over Dillicar troughs in the Lune Gorge by Hughes 2-6-0 No 2893 — a postwar scene.

Above: Amongst the Derbyshire limestone, Hughes 2-6-0 No 2845 pulls hard on the rising gradient in Chee Dale on a spring day just after the war.

Left: Also in Chee Dale, one of Fowler's successful 2-6-4Ts, No 2372, emerges from a tunnel on this ex-Midland main line.

Above right: Stanier 2-6-2T No 98 on the Morecambe-Carnforth route exchanges the single-line token at Hest Bank in August 1946.

Below right: Veteran 0-6-2 'Coal Tank' No 7711 of F. W. Webb's long-running series takes water at Edge Hill shed in July 1939.

L M S
9B

L M S

Above: Another of these fussy little engines, No 7803, handles a Bolton (Great Moor Street) to Manchester Exchange stopping train near Roe Green in 1944.

Below: LNWR 0-6-2T No 6931 (of a class sometimes nicknamed 'Bashers') takes on fuel at the Edge Hill coaling stage in July 1939.

Above: Ex-LNWR 0-8-0 No 9203 passes Carnforth No 1 signalbox as it draws out on to the main line from the Carnforth refuge sidings with a southbound goods.

Below: Impressive in repose, rebuilt 'Claughton' No 5946 *Duke of Connaught* is ready to leave Edge Hill shed to go back to work in 1939.

Above: Ex-LNWR superheated 'Precursor' No 25292 *Medusa* backs off Patricroft shed at Eccles Junction en route to Manchester Exchange to pick up a train (photograph taken about 1937).

Below: Bowen-Cooke 4-6-2T No 6979 stands by in Tebay yard in August 1939 ready to give banking assistance up Shap.

Above: Ex-LNWR 0-8-0 No 9302 travels with a 'Wrong Line Order' past relaying at Roe Green just after the war.

Below: Saddle tanks at Edge Hill: an ex-LNWR 0-6-0T No 27309 and LMS 0-4-0T No 7002, a much later example of this type of locomotive. No 7002 was built by Kitson's for the LMSR in 1932 for dock shunting and colliery lines with severe curvature.

Above: No 7892, seen at Patricroft, was one of the very few ex-LNWR 0-8-2Ts still in service in August 1946.

Below: A heavy northbound train of oil tank wagons is seen near Golborne in August 1946 with ex-LNWR 0-8-0 No 9304 at the head.

Above: Ex-LNWR 19in Goods No 8801 shunts in the colliery siding at Astley Green in June 1946. Only three of this class, one of them being 8801, survived to the date of Nationalisation, 18 months later, and all were scrapped by 1950 still carrying their LMS numbers.

Below: Roe Green recedes behind a smokescreen as ex-LNWR 0-8-0 No 8962 gets to grips with a long coal train in June 1947.

Above: In the shadow of Nationalisation ex-LNWR 'Coal Tank' No 7803 still earns its keep on the Bolton (Great Moor Street) and Manchester Exchange service, passing Roe Green with characteristic bustle.

Below: A Warrington to St Helens local passes Winwick in June 1946 headed by ex-LNWR 2-4-2T No 6663.

Above: Running light, No 6812, ex-LNWR 'Precursor' 4-4-2T, waits for signals at Hest Bank in June 1939.

Below: In the immediate aftermath of World War II an unidentified 'Patriot' on an up train passes Winwick at high speed on the falling gradient to Warrington, its appearance reflecting wartime austerity.

Above: 'Patriot' Class 4-6-0 No 5516 *The Hertfordshire and Bedfordshire Regiment* passes Hest Bank in July 1942 with a Preston train.

Below: After a rapid descent from Shap summit, 'Jubilee' No 5635 *Tobago* crosses the River Lune just south of Tebay and enters the Lune Gorge in July 1947.

Top and above: Two views of 'Patriots' which were often employed on the late afternoon postwar Manchester Exchange to Barrow service. No 5502 *The Royal Naval Division* is at Roe Green, and No 5505 *The Royal Army Ordnance Corps* near Worsley.

Left: Stanier 'Black Five' No 5189 climbs away from Lancaster on a southbound freight in the postwar period.

Right: Midland Class 4 0-6-0 No 4147 storms into Millers Dale station on an August day in 1947.

Below: Passing permanent way repairs at Sandersons Sidings, Roe Green, Class 5 No 5199 picks its way with caution.

Far right, above: Streamlined Pacific No 6225 *Duchess of Gloucester* re-starts a heavy Glasgow-bound train out of Carlisle Citadel station on a wet day in August 1939.

Far right, below: Another streamlined Pacific, No 6228 *Duchess of Rutland*, heads for the north at Golborne with a 15-coach train in August 1946.

W63

Above: Camera and photographer about to get rather wet as No 6234 *Duchess of Abercorn* takes up more than enough water from Dillicar troughs, Tebay, in July 1947. The photograph shows the effect of smoke deflectors when travelling at high speed.

Below: Pacifics did not appear on the LMS until Stanier's 'Princess Royal' class emerged from Crewe in 1933. Here No 6208 *Princess Helena Victoria* heads a long up train at speed through Acton Bridge station in the summer of 1946.

Above: A little further north, No 6211 *Queen Maud* lifts a heavy train up the rising gradient at Preston Brook, south of Warrington, in August 1947.

Below: The ultimate in motive power on the LMS was the Stanier 'Coronation' class; No 6231 *Duchess of Atholl* is seen here in July 1938 leaving Carnforth for the north. At the time, this locomotive was fitted with the original single chimney.

Above: Because of a serious accident on the main line at Winsford, the 'Royal Scot', headed by No 6233 *Duchess of Sutherland*, is seen at Roe Green. The train had been diverted via Manchester London Road, Castlefield and Eccles Junction and was making its way north to join the West Coast main line again at Wigan.

Below: 'Coronation' class No 6223 Princess Alice makes a smoky start from Carnforth in August 1947.

Top: Still retaining its streamlining in late 1947, 'Coronration' class No 6240 *City of Coventry* passes Golborne at high speed with a down train of 17 coaches.

Above: No 6100 *Royal Scot*, still carrying the bell fitted when the locomotive toured America and Canada in 1933, ascends Shap with a mixed train near Shap Wells in July 1938.

Below: No banking assistance required on this occasion as 'Jubilee' No 5715 *Invincible* and 'Royal Scot' No 6163 *Civil Service Rifleman* haul a heavy train up Shap in 1938. With safety valves blowing almost at the summit, they are taking the climb in their stride.

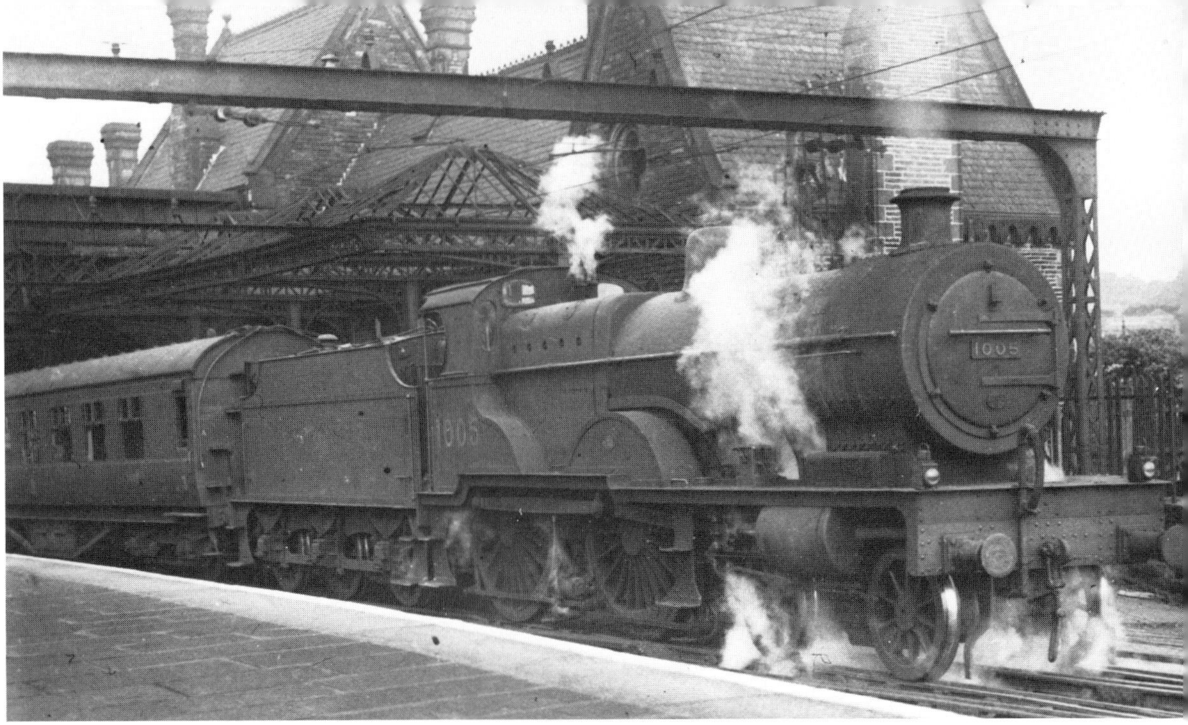

Above: Midland Compound No 1005, seen here at Lancaster Green Ayre station, shows signs of poor postwar maintenance.

Below: An LMS development of the Midland Compound built by Vulcan Foundry, No 1187 approaches Walkden troughs with a local train on the former L&Y Manchester to Liverpool route in April 1945.

Above: Outside Carnforth LNWR shed in May 1938, Compound No 1162 awaits its next turn of duty.

Below: Sunshine and shadow in Manchester London Road station just after the war as Compound No 1122 marshals coaches for a local train.

Above: Compound No 1120 works an up train near Hest Bank in July 1938.

Below: No 691, an LMS development of the Midland Class 2 4-4-0, takes water from Walkden troughs as it heads a Manchester to Southport train in July 1939.

Above: 'Royal Scot' No 6149 *The Middlesex Regiment* is assisted by Class 2 No 489 on a heavy southbound train near Euxton in July 1938.

Below: Class 2 No 654 stands at the manually operated coaling stage at Tebay in June 1939.

Above: Rebuilt Johnson Class 2 No 397 takes water from Dillicar troughs, piloting 'Black Five' No 5309 in August 1947.

Below: Ex-MR 2-4-0 No 20185 shunts at Upperby in the summer of 1939.

Above: Another Midland survivor 0-4-4T No 1278 works the Millers Dale to Buxton branch in August 1947.

Below: Two noisy ex-L&Y Horwich-built engines pass Moorside & Wardly with a Manchester train in June 1941. Aspinall 0-6-0 No 12296 pilots 2-4-2T No 10822.

Above: A Barton Wright 0-6-0 built in 1887 poses with its crew at Patricroft mpd in August 1946.

Below: Ex-L&Y Hughes large-boilered 0-8-0 No 12948 works a Wigan-bound goods train at Moorside in May 1939.

Above: Another scene at Moorside as a lengthy goods train is ably handled by ex-L&Y 0-6-0 No 12517.

Below: Hughes L&Y 0-8-0 No 12952 on shed at Newton Heath.

Above left: A local train hurrying past Moorside in the spring of 1945 is headed by ex-L&Y 2-4-2T No 10823.

Below left: The LMS standard design of 0-6-0T shunting engine (the 'Jinty') was a development of the MR 7200 class. No 7524 stands at Crewe station (and is carrying express passenger headlamp code!).

Above: Horwich 'Crab' 2-6-0 No 2920 climbs Shap with a heavy goods train banked by 0-8-0 No 9035 in May 1939.

Below: Ivatt 2-6-0 No 6418 stands idle at Newton Heath shed yard in the postwar era.

Above: A Fairburn 2-6-4T is prepared for duty at Newton Heath shed.

Right: Stanier 2-cylinder 2-6-4T No 2454 leaves Worsley station with a Manchester to Tydesley train in April 1944.

Right: On a similar turn of duty, No 2561 takes its train past Roe Green junction in June 1947.

Below: Stanier 'Black Five' No 5296 takes the Manchester (Liverpool Road) to Carlisle goods past Sandersons Sidings, Worsley, on a June evening in 1947.

Above: 'Jubilee' No 5686 *St Vincent* tops the summit at Golborne with a heavy train of vans in the summer of 1946.

Below: Cold morning air creates a grand steam effect as LMS Class 4 0-6-0 No 4060 leaves Hest Bank with a stopping train for Carlisle in May 1945.

Above: Both tender and firebox of ex-MR Class 3F 0-6-0 No 3389 are well filled with coal on passing Winwick in July 1946, ready for the climb to Golborne summit with a northbound goods.

Below: Coaling the hard way! Class 4F 0-6-0 No 4469 has its tender replenished at the Tebay coaling stage in July 1947.

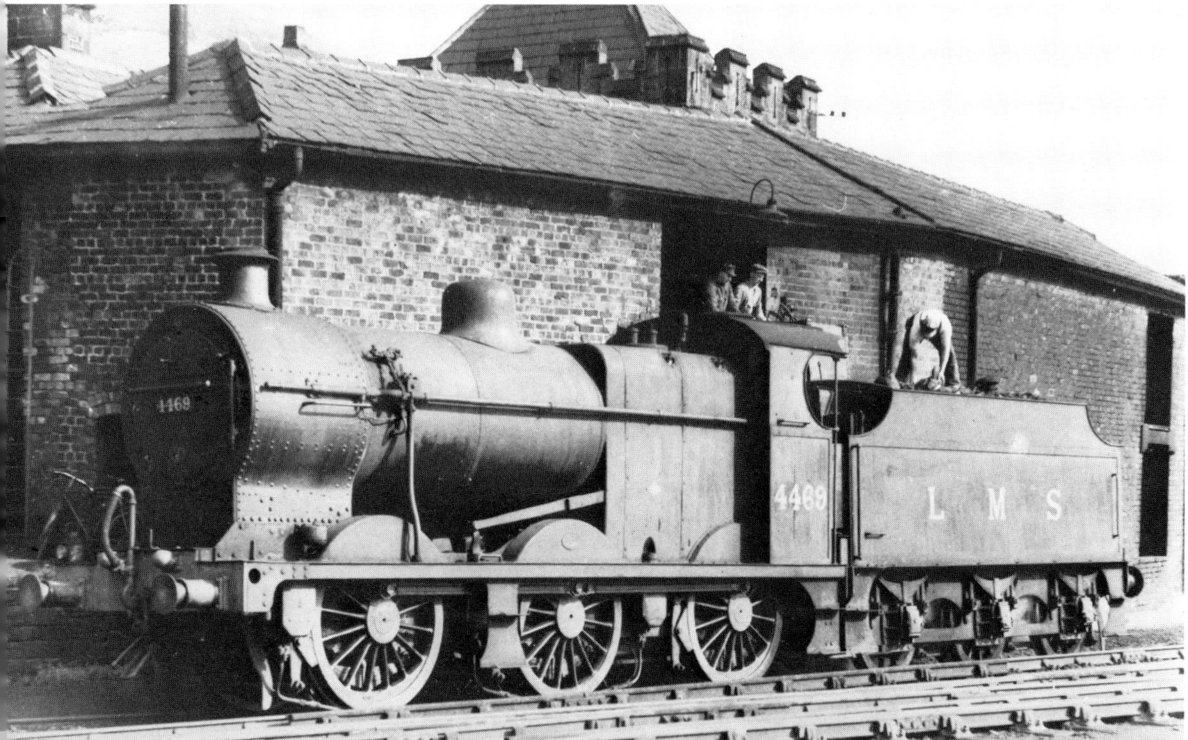

Above: Class 4F 0-6-0 No 4349 heads south at the bottom of Shap in June 1939 with a train of empty wagons approaching the junction at Tebay with the LNER Kirkby Stephen line, seen curving to the right.

Below: Class 4F 0-6-0 No 4421 makes a smoky entrance to Preston station from the north with a Special in 1939. The Blackpool lines are in the foreground.

Above: Another Class 4F No 4504, pilots a Class 5 on a mixed freight train surmounting the summit at Golborne in the Spring of 1945.

Below: Two 'Black Fives' arrive at Sandersons Sidings, Worsley, ready to take up their turns of duty.

Top: Fowler 2-6-2T No 58 passes Roe Green with a Manchester-Bolton (Great Moor Street) train just after the war.

Above: A mixed freight approaches Tebay headed by Fowler 2-6-2T No 21 in July 1947.

Below: Fowler 2-6-2T No 15 is ready to move off, from Newton Heath shed yard (a postwar scene).

Above: One of the rather short-lived Fowler 0-8-0 Class 7F engines ('Austin Sevens'), No 9667, at Newton Heath just after the war.

Below: Starting on a journey over the Pennines in July 1947, this Fowler 0-8-0, No 9643, makes a bold effort at Newton Heath.

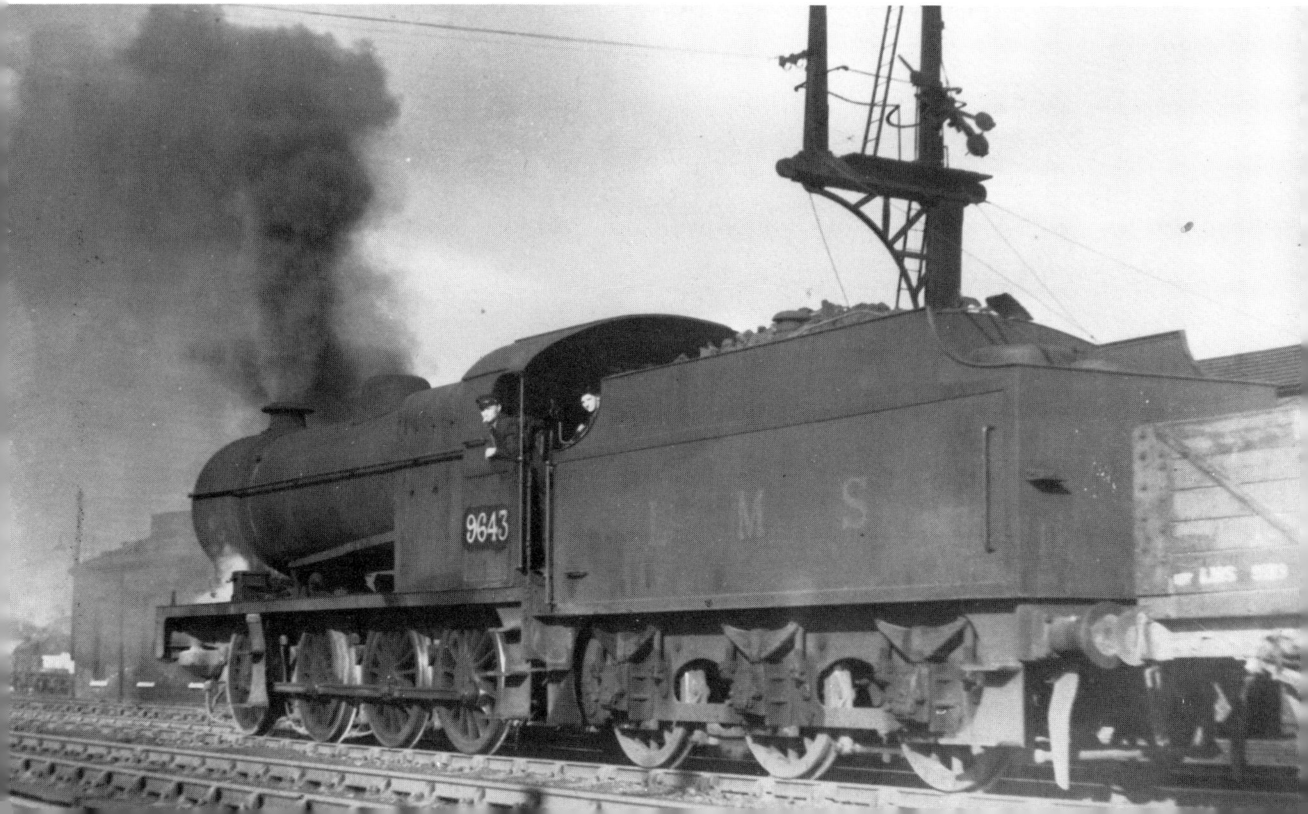

Above: One of five Fowler 0-8-0s modified for oil-burning, No 9670 at Newton Heath shed. Four were scrapped in 1949 shortly after the railways were nationalised and not long after this photograph was taken. Only No 9511 was converted back for coal burning.

Below: Another Fowler 0-8-0 at Newton Heath No 9666.

Above: Another postwar scene at Newton Heath shows 0-8-0s Nos 9565 and 9667 on the ash plant.

Below: Ex-LNWR 0-6-0 'Cauliflower' No 28345 on the Stafford turntable just outside the Bagnall Locomotive Works ('Cauliflower' refers to the supposed resemblance to that vegetable of the LNWR coat of arms on the splasher).

Above: Ex-LNWR 'Prince of Wales' class No 25673 *Lusitania* at Stafford. Once a main line express locomotive, this is pictured performing a very menial task in the last year of its life.

Below: Gently easing a 56-wagon train of coal down the falling gradient past Sandersons Sidings, Worsley, is ex-LNWR 0-8-0 No 9134.

Above: Another LNWR 0-8-0 No 9085 makes a smoky passage through Worsley station in postwar years.

Below: Stanier Class 5 No 5402 at Ellenbrook in October 1947 moves a rake of empty wagons down the falling gradient towards Patricroft.

Above: A further example of 'how the mighty are fallen!' One of the remaining ex-L&Y Hughes 4-6-0 'Dreadnought' class No 10448 takes a freight train through Preston station in August 1947.

Below: Ex-L&Y 0-6-0 No 12466 ambles past Sandhole Colliery, Wardley, at the point where the M62 Motorway now crosses what remains of the line. The fast lines were lifted at the end of the steam era and little traffic now passes.

Top: An ex-L&Y Hughes 4-6-0 draws a Liverpool train out of Preston station in August 1947.

Above and below: Two photographs taken during World War II at Moorside show ex-L&Y locomotives in charge of freight trains — 0-6-0 No 12124 and 0-8-0 No 12838.

Above: Ex-L&Y Aspinall 0-4-0T No 11234 belongs to one of the smallest classes of locomotives on the LMS, designed for light shunting on lines with sharp curvature.

Below: An ex-works Aspinall 0-6-0, No 12219 at Moorside is in radiant condition after repainting.

Above: Horwich ex-L&Y 'Crab' No 2868 leaves Preston shed to take a local train in February 1945.

Below: Ex-LNWR 0-8-0 No 9311, still retaining its original chimney, heads a freight train just south of Hest Bank station in May 1945.

Above left: Those were really 'LMS Days' — the days of the 'Coronation Scot' (popularly known as the 'Blue Train'). In July 1938 streamlined 'Coronation' class Stanier Pacific No 6221 *Queen Elizabeth* hustles the up 'Coronation Scot' southwards from Shap, accelerating rapidly down the gradient.

Centre left: Eight years later, at Golborne, No 6221 is pictured again but without the streamlined casing. The casing impeded maintenance, and removal from this class commenced in 1946, the year of this photograph. The engine still retains its sloping smokebox.

Below left: After descending Shap, 'Coronation' class Pacific No 6243 *City of Lancaster* flashes past Tebay No 2 Box at high speed, crossing the junction with the LNER Kirkby Stephen line at the north end of the station.

Above: 'Royal Scot' No 6155 *The Lancer* hurries a southbound train across Dillicar troughs in the Lune Gorge in August 1947.

Below: When first introduced in 1927, the 'Royal Scot' class ran without smoke deflectors as shown in this view of No 6117 *Welsh Guardsman* taken about 1928. The author is leaning against Penrith up starter signal post as he admires the outside motion of this new class of locomotive.

Above: 'Royal Scot' No 6148 *The Manchester Regiment* rests appropriately in the Manchester area at Longsight shed on an April day in 1938.

Below: A raft of 'dead' engines is moved by an ex-LNWR 0-8-0 from Crewe Works into Crewe North shed on a day in July 1938. 'Jubilee' No 5591 *Udaipur* and 'Royal Scot' No 6150 *The Life Guardsman* were in company with an unidentified 'Jubilee'.

Above: 'Royal Scot' No 6159 *The Royal Air Force* reaches the last lap of the climb from Penrith to Shap summit in July 1938.

Below: Rebuilt 'Royal Scot' No 6104 *Scottish Borderer* races through Tebay station with an up train on a rather dull summer day in 1947, the appearance of the locomotive in keeping with the weather.

Above: Ready for a return to service, 'Royal Scot' No 6112 *Sherwood Forester* sparkles at Crewe South shed in April 1939 after a general overhaul in Crewe Works.

Below: Heading a stopping train, 'Royal Scot' No 6122 *Royal Ulster Rifleman* gets on the move after a stop at Carnforth in May 1938.

Above: 'Patriot' class No 5516 *The Hertfordshire and Bedfordshire Regiment* looms above the miscellany of coaches forming this up train at Brock just after World War II.

Below: 'Patriot' No 5533 *Lord Rathmore* works a local train into Grayrigg station in June 1939.

Above: Although the first of the 'Patriots' to be withdrawn from service, No 5502 *Royal Naval Division* had many years of service before it when this portrait was taken at Edge Hill in October 1938.

Below: Odd man out No 6202 was the only example of a turbine-driven locomotive in this country to have a working life of reasonable length (1935-1952, mostly on London-Liverpool diagrams). She was rebuilt in 1952 with reciprocating propulsion but had a very short life in that form, being scrapped after involvement in the disastrous accident at Harrow. The photograph was taken at Edge Hill in 1939.

Above: A Manchester-Blackpool businessman's express passes Moorside headed by 'Jubilee' No 5698 *Mars* about 1947.

Below: 'Jubilee' class No 5690 *Leander* (now preserved) pilots Pacific No 6253 *City of St Albans* on a London-bound express passing through Tebay station at high speed in July 1947.

Above: 'Jubilee' No 5718 *Dreadnought* climbs Grayrigg bank with a down freight on a midsummer day in 1947.

Below: Pictured here in June 1938 at Longsight coaling stage, 'Jubilee' No 5611 *Hong Kong* has a straight-sided tender not commonly seen with this class of engine.

Above: 'Jubilee' No 5711 *Courageous* at Newton Heath shed about 1947 is fitted with an LMS (Fowler) 3,500gall tender.

Below: This ex-LNWR 0-8-0 No 9230 still carried the LNWR pattern chimney when photographed approaching Tebay in July 1947, ready to start the hard slog up Shap with banking assistance.

Above: F. W. Webb's LNWR 0-6-2 'Coal Tanks' did much good work over the Manchester, Bolton and Tyldesley lines. No 7799 is seen here at Ellenbrook in October 1947.

Below: Another 'Coal Tank' No 7720 approaches Earlestown with a local from Warrington, about 1947.

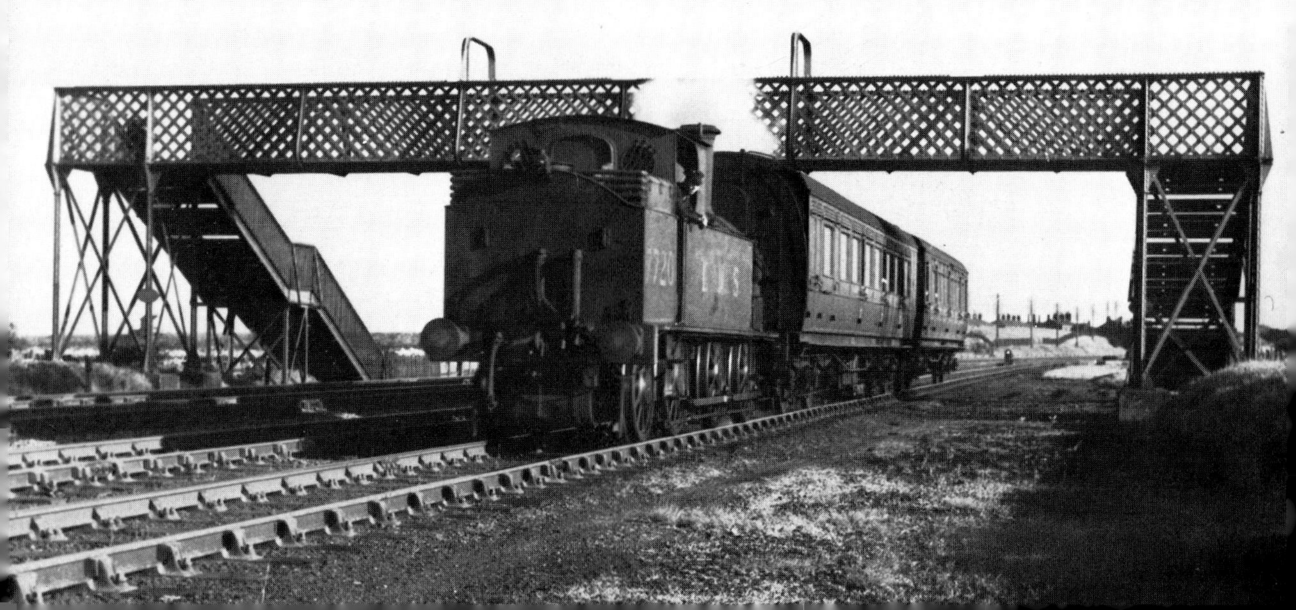

Above: This ex-LNWR 0-8-4T No 7957, photographed at Edge Hill about 1938, belonged to a class of engine not popular with footplate staff.

Below: A lengthy freight train clatters southwards behind ex-LNWR 0-8-0 No 9255, seen passing through Garstang & Catterall station about 1947.

Above: 'Patriot' (unofficially known as 'Baby Scot') class No 5537 *Private E. Sykes VC* waits at Preston to move down to the station on a wet and misty day in February 1945.

Below: Ex-MR 0-6-0 No 3630 trails a long white cloud over its westbound freight at Moorside.

Above: Excursions were a frequent duty for Class 4 freight 0-6-0s. No 4398 is near Euxton on such a train in 1938.

Below: Another Class 4 0-6-0, No 4448, hauls a heavy freight train through Moorside in World War II days.

Above left: Ex-MR 0-6-0 No 3305 at Edge Hill shed in July 1939 represents the classic freight type of an earlier age.

Below left: A Class 4 freight 0-6-0 at Tebay in June 1939 waits to return to its home shed in Barrow.

Above: Class 5 4-6-0 No 5494 passes Hest Bank with an up freight train about 1947.

Below: Making an all-out effort, 'Black Five' No 5398 nears the summit of Shap in July 1938 with a down freight.

Above: Class 5 4-6-0 No 5039 leaves Hest Bank with an up stopping train in August 1947.

Below: A local train heading for Preston ambles along the main line at Bolton-le-Sands, near Carnforth, in April 1945 behind 2-6-4T No 2428.

Above: Improved carrying capacity compared with the Fowler Midland pattern tender was provided by 4,000gal units designed by Stanier; 2-8-0 No 8665 draws water at Stafford.

Below: LMS Compound 4-4-0 No 1098 works a Chester to Manchester via Tyldesley train about 1946, and is seen near Tyldesley.

Above: A long southbound freight headed by Class 5 4-6-0 No 5064 runs through Hest Bank station in the immediate aftermath of World War II.

Below: Just west of Chinley, on the Midland main line, ex-Midland rebuilt Johnson Class 2 4-4-0 No 461 takes a train past Buxworth in 1938.

Above: Still with its original handsome Derby chimney, LMS Fowler Class 2 4-4-0 No 585 runs into Preston station with a train from Blackpool in July 1939.

Below: Class 5 4-6-0 No 5451 makes a very unspectacular approach to Carnforth with an up freight in May 1938.

Above: A photograph redolent of the peak of the LMS days, epitomising the power, speed and prestige implicit in the name of the company. The first of W. A. Stanier's streamlined 'Coronation' class Pacifics No 6220 *Coronation* thunders up Shap in 1938 with the down 'Coronation Scot'. Those were the days!
Below: Mr W. D. Cooper with some of the small-power steam locomotives he has built. Three well known designs pictured in this book are seen, together with a freelance 2-6-2.